SUPER SIMPLE BODY

INSIDE THE SKIN, HAIR & NAILS

KARIN HALVORSON, M.D.

Consulting Editor, Diane Craig, M.A./Reading Specialist

Super Sandcastle

An Imprint of Abdo Publishing
abdopublishing.com

VISIT US AT ABDOPUBLISHING.COM

Published by Abdo Publishing, a division of ABDO, PO Box 398166, Minneapolis, Minnesota 55439. Copyright © 2016 by Abdo Consulting Group, Inc. International copyrights reserved in all countries. No part of this book may be reproduced in any form without written permission from the publisher. Super SandCastle™ is a trademark and logo of Abdo Publishing.

Printed in the United States of America,
North Mankato, Minnesota
102015
012016

Editor: Liz Salzmann
Content Developer: Nancy Tuminelly
Cover and Interior Design: Mighty Media, Inc.
Photo Credits: Shutterstock

Library of Congress Cataloging-in-Publication Data
Halvorson, Karin, 1979- author.
  Inside the skin, hair & nails / Karin Halvorson, M.D. ; consulting editor, Diane Craig, M.A./reading specialist.
    pages cm. -- (Super simple body)
  ISBN 978-1-62403-942-3
1. Skin--Juvenile literature. 2. Hair--Juvenile literature. 3. Fingernails--Juvenile literature. I. Title. II. Title: Inside the skin, hair and nails. III. Series: Halvorson, Karin, 1979- Super simple body.
  QP88.5.H27 2016
  612.7'9--dc23
                    2015020588

Super SandCastle™ books are created by a team of professional educators, reading specialists, and content developers around five essential components—phonemic awareness, phonics, vocabulary, text comprehension, and fluency—to assist young readers as they develop reading skills and strategies and increase their general knowledge. All books are written, reviewed, and leveled for guided reading and early reading intervention programs for use in shared, guided, and independent reading and writing activities to support a balanced approach to literacy instruction.

NOTE TO ADULTS

THIS BOOK is all about encouraging children to learn the science of how their bodies work! Be there to help make science fun and interesting for young readers. Many activities are included in this book to help children further explore what they've learned. Some require adult assistance and/ or permission. Make sure children have appropriate places where they can do the activities safely.

Children may also have questions about what they've learned. Offer help and guidance when they have questions. Most of all, encourage them to keep exploring and learning new things!

CONTENTS

YOUR BODY

YOUR HAIR

YOUR SKIN

YOUR NAILS

You're amazing! So is your body!
Your body has a lot of different parts. Your
kidneys, skin, blood, muscles, and bones
all work together every day. They keep you
moving. Even when you don't realize it.

Do you know what your body's biggest organ is? It's skin! Every animal has skin. It protects everything inside your body. Skin holds everything together.

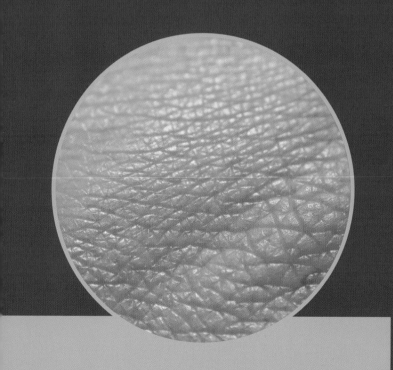

WHAT CAN YOU FEEL?

ALL ABOUT THE
SKIN

Skin has a lot of jobs. It keeps your insides in place. It does a lot of other things too.

Touch It!

Skin helps you feel the world. It sends signals to your brain when you touch things!

Layer on Layer

Skin is made up of layers. Each layer has millions of tiny cells.

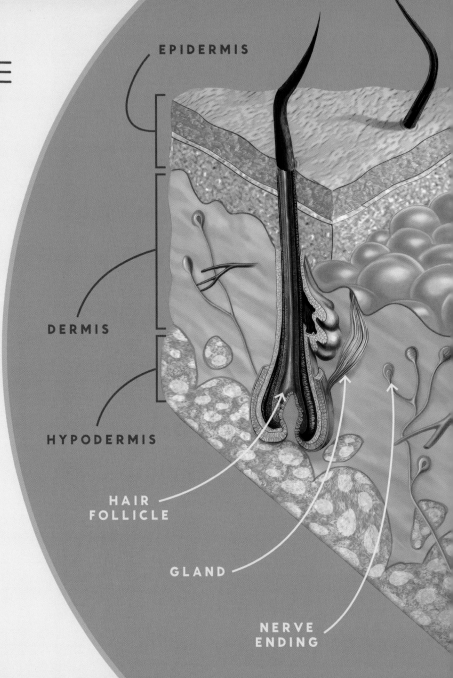

EPIDERMIS

DERMIS

HYPODERMIS

HAIR FOLLICLE

GLAND

NERVE ENDING

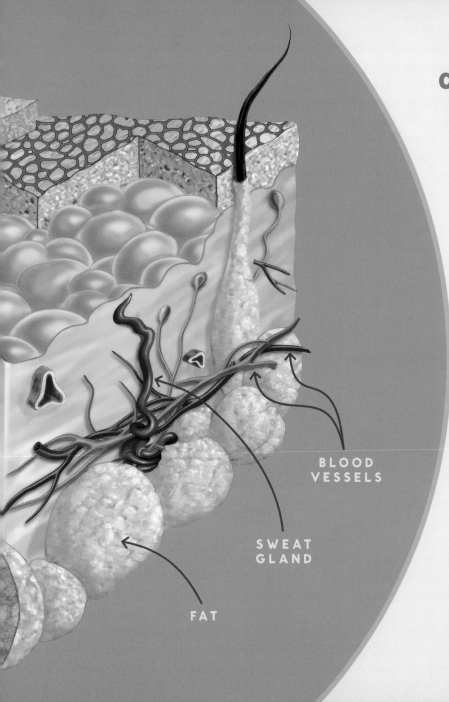

BLOOD
VESSELS

SWEAT
GLAND

FAT

Comfy or Cool?

Skin makes sure your body is the right temperature. Skin sweats when you are hot. This helps you cool down.

Skin gets goose bumps when you are cold. This helps you warm up.

THE
TOP
LAYER

The top layer of the skin is the epidermis (*ep-i-DUR-mis*). It is what you see when you look at your skin.

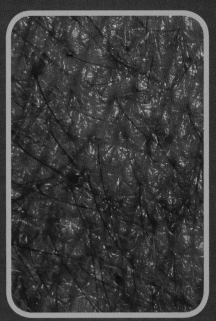

EPIDERMIS

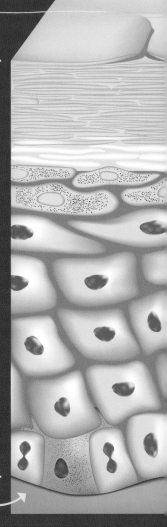

DERMIS

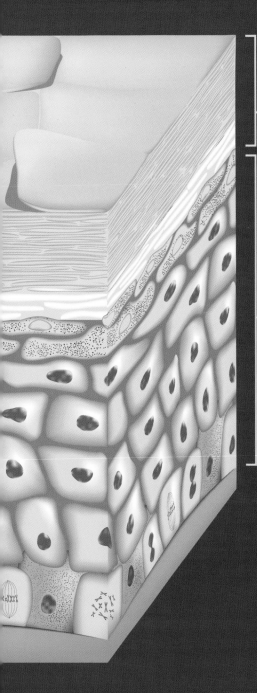

DEAD
CELLS

LIVING
CELLS

Your epidermis covers your body. But it doesn't stick around. It flakes off. You lose 30,000 skin cells every hour! But your skin won't wear out. It is always growing.

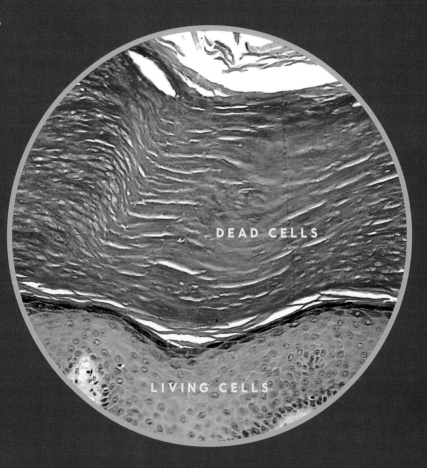

DEAD CELLS

LIVING CELLS

EPIDERMIS

THE MIDDLE LAYER

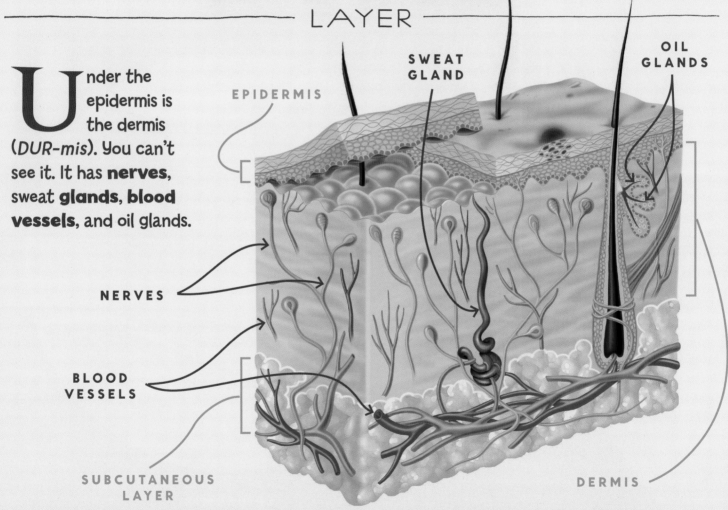

Under the epidermis is the dermis (*DUR-mis*). You can't see it. It has **nerves**, sweat **glands, blood vessels,** and oil glands.

EPIDERMIS

SWEAT GLAND

OIL GLANDS

NERVES

BLOOD VESSELS

SUBCUTANEOUS LAYER

DERMIS

NERVES in your dermis connect to your brain. They tell you what your skin is touching. When you touch something hot, your dermis tells your brain to move.

SWEAT GLANDS and **BLOOD VESSELS** work together. Sweat glands cool you down. Blood vessels keep you warm.

OIL GLANDS keep your skin **waterproof.**

THE BOTTOM LAYER

The third layer of your skin is made of fat. It is called the subcutaneous (*suhb-kyoo-TEY-nee-uhs*) layer. It keeps you warm. It provides padding when you fall too.

EPIDERMIS
(FIRST LAYER)

DERMIS
(SECOND LAYER)

SUBCUTANEOUS
(THIRD LAYER)

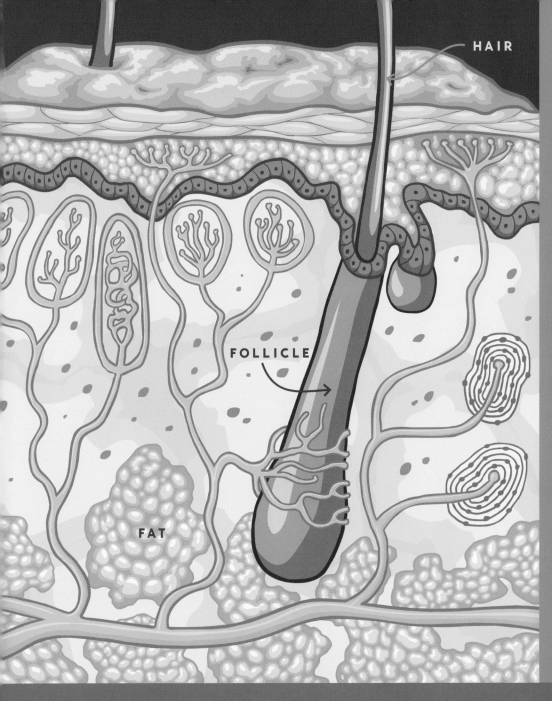

HAIR

FOLLICLE

FAT

Hair grows out of the fat layer. It grows out of special tubes called follicles (*FOL-i-kuhlz*). They are all over your body.

HAIR

EVERYWHERE

Hair is made of keratin (*KAIR-uh tin*). It grows almost everywhere on your body! The hair in some places is thick. It is easy to see. The hair in other places is very thin. It is hard to see.

Some types of hair have special jobs. Eyelash hair keeps dust out of your eyes. Eyebrow hair keeps sweat off your face. The hair on your head and arms keeps you warm.

No hair grows on your lips, **palms**, or the bottoms of your feet.

  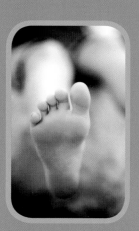

Hairy Facts

You have 5 million hairs on your body!

You lose 50 to 100 hairs from your head every day.

Each hair grows 2 to 6 years before falling out.

EDIBLE SKIN

MAKE SOME SKIN YOU CAN EAT!

WHAT YOU NEED: GLASS BAKING DISH, MINI MARSHMALLOWS, BOWL, SPOON, RED GELATIN, PLATE, FRUIT LEATHER, BLACK STRING LICORICE, RULER, KNIFE

HOW TO DO IT

1. Make a layer of marshmallows in the baking dish.

2. Put the gelatin in a bowl. Add water according to the directions on the box. Pour the gelatin over the marshmallows. The marshmallows will float to the top. Put the dish in the refrigerator for 2 hours.

3. Cut out a square of gelatin. Put it marshmallow-side down on a plate.

4. Cover the gelatin with a layer of fruit leather.

5. Cut licorice into 1-inch (2.5 cm) pieces. Lay the licorice pieces on top of the fruit leather.

WHAT'S HAPPENING?

The marshmallows are the subcutaneous layer of skin. The gelatin is the dermis. The fruit leather is the epidermis. The licorice pieces are the hair that grows out of skin.

FINGERPRINTS

Y ou have a series of tiny **ridges** on each fingertip. They formed before you were born.

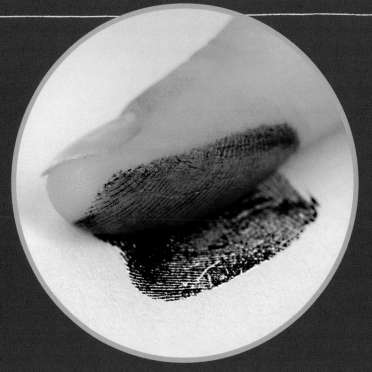

Your fingers have sweat and oils on them. When you touch something, you leave a print behind. It is in the shape of the ridges. It is called a fingerprint.

Everyone's fingerprints are different!

Types of Fingerprints

ARCH
The **ridges** slope
up and down.

WHORL
The ridges make
a circle.

LOOP
The ridges make
a loop.

SCIENCE DETECTIVE

FIND YOUR FINGERPRINTS!

WHAT YOU NEED: PENCIL, RULER, 2 SHEETS OF PAPER, CLEAR TAPE

HOW TO DO IT

1. Draw a 2-inch (5 cm) square on a sheet of paper. Fill it in with the pencil.

2. Rub your finger on the square.

3. Press a piece of tape over your finger. Pull it off. Put the tape on the second sheet of paper.

WHAT'S HAPPENING?

The pencil lead stuck to the **ridges** on your finger. It came off on the tape. It made a fingerprint. What type of fingerprint do you have? Try it with your friends and family members.

TOUGH AS NAILS

N ails grow from roots under your skin. The root is behind your cuticle (*KYOO-ti-kuhl*). Your cuticle is the U-shape at the bottom of each nail.

Nails protect your fingertips and toes. They are made of keratin, like hair. They never stop growing.

FINGERNAIL

CUTICLE

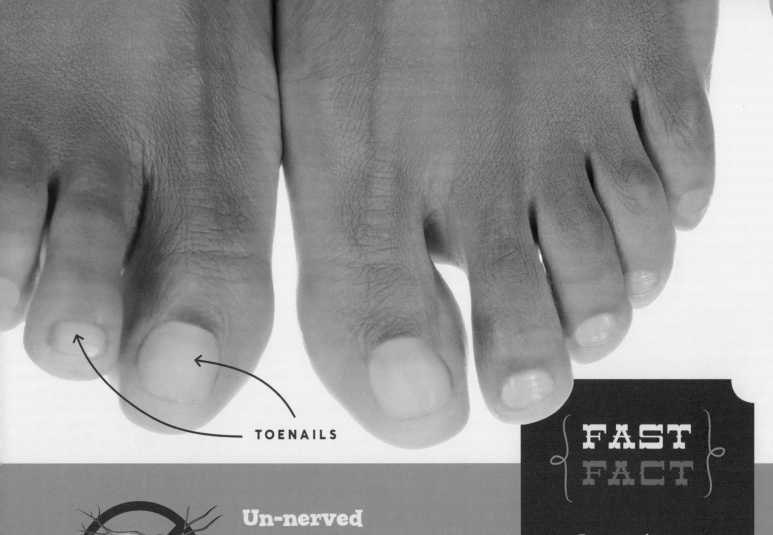

TOENAILS

Un-nerved

You can't feel pain in your nails. They don't have **nerve** endings. That's why it doesn't hurt when you cut your nails.

Fingernails grow four times faster than toenails.

SUPER

SENSES

HOW GOOD ARE YOUR SENSES?

WHAT YOU NEED: YARN, STRING, THREAD, RULER, SCISSORS, 3 CRAFT STICKS, MARKER, TAPE, BLINDFOLD

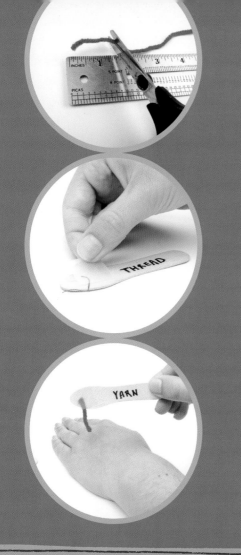

HOW TO DO IT

1. Cut 1-inch (2.5 cm) pieces of yarn, string, and thread.

2. Label the craft sticks "yarn," "string," and "thread." Tape each **strand** to the correct craft stick.

3. Put on a blindfold. Have a friend slowly touch the thread to the back of your hand. Your friend should press until the strand bends a little. Repeat with the other strands.

4. Which type of strand was easiest to feel?

5. Switch places with your friend! Test other parts of your arm.

WHAT'S HAPPENING?

Your skin has many **nerve** endings in some spots. In those spots you can feel the strands more easily.

SKIN
COLOR

Skin comes in many colors. Melanin (*MEL-uh-nin*) gives skin its color. More melanin makes skin darker.

Melanin keeps your skin from burning. Your skin makes melanin when you are in the sun. You get tan. Sometimes it can't make enough. Then you get a sunburn!

Hair comes in many colors too. It also has melanin. Melanin gives your hair its color. When people get old they lose melanin. Their hair turns gray.

Where Do Freckles Come From?

Melanin is spread out in your skin. Sometimes it clumps together. When you go in the sun, the clumps turn red or brown. They become freckles.

THE POWER OF SUNSCREEN

SAVE YOUR SKIN!

WHAT YOU NEED: BLACK CONSTRUCTION PAPER, PENCIL, SUNSCREEN, PAINTBRUSH, SUN, PAPER TOWEL

HOW TO DO IT

1. Fold the construction paper in half. Unfold it.

2. Label one half of the paper "skin." Label the other half of the paper "sunscreen." Paint **sunscreen** on the "sunscreen" half.

3. Lay the paper in the sun. Leave it there for the day.

4. Gently rub the sunscreen off with a wet paper **towel**.

WHAT'S HAPPENING?

The side with sunscreen stayed darker. The sunscreen protected the paper from the sun. The sun made the color on the unprotected side fade.

29

KEEP IT CLEAN

Being clean keeps you healthy. It also makes your skin, hair, and nails look better.

Wash Up

Wash your skin every day with soap and water. Washing gets rid of dead skin. Use **sunscreen** when you go outside. It keeps your skin from burning.

Nail Care

Cut your fingernails and toenails.
If your nails are too long you can
scratch yourself.

Hair Care

Wash your hair with shampoo.
It removes sweat and dirt.

GLOSSARY

BLOOD VESSEL – one of the tubes that carry blood throughout the body.

GLAND – an organ in the body that makes chemicals your body needs.

KIDNEY – an organ in the body that turns waste from the blood into urine.

NERVE – one of the threads in the body that takes messages to and from the brain.

PALM – the inside of your hand between your wrist and fingers.

RIDGE – a narrow, raised area on the surface of something.

STRAND – a thin object, such as a hair, string, or wire.

SUNSCREEN – something you rub on your skin to keep the sun from burning it.

TOWEL – a cloth or paper used for cleaning or drying.

WATERPROOF – able to keep water out.